Fantasy Designs

First published in Great Britain 2012 by

Search Press Limited
Wellwood
North Farm Road
Tunbridge Wells
Kent TN2 3DR

Text copyright © Search Press 2012
Photographs by Debbie Patterson,
Search Press Studios
Photographs and design copyright ©
Search Press Ltd 2012

ISBN: 978-1-84448-624-3

The Complete Book of Fantasy Designs is a
compendium volume of illustrations taken from
the Design Source Books: *Halloween Designs*,
Christmas Designs, *Angel and Fairy Designs*
and *Mythical Creatures*.

Printed in Malaysia

Page 1
Dragon Plaque
Design, see page 84
*This spectacular dragon plaque, made from polymer clay,
would make a dramatic impact in any room. Painted in
warm colours and metallic wax, it shimmers in the light,
giving the impression that a stream of flames might
appear from the dragon's mouth at any moment! (see
page 13).*

Page 2
Party Mask
Design, see page 26
*Remain a mystery in this theatrical mask – perfect for
parties (see page 7).*

Page 3
Sophisticated Star Box
Design, see page 26
*This paper mâché box is given an ethereal feel by
decorating it with a swirl of stars, punched from silver card.
It is layered with torn pieces of silver tissue paper and a
PVA glue and water solution – as the tissue dries, it creates
a wonderful textured surface. It's the perfect container in
which to present a gift or store your bits and pieces or
simply to display in your home (see page 14).*

Contents

Introduction

Fantasy art is a genre that depicts the magical and the supernatural – from beautiful, ethereal creatures to monstrous and terrifying beasts. The designs in this book include an eclectic mix of themes, which merge elements from fairy tales, horror, and ancient myths and legends. Dragons, mermaids, wizards, witches, fairies, goblins, pixies and other mythical creatures are common features in fantasy art, and they come alive as they dance across these pages, so you're sure to find plenty to spark your imagination. Other designs include flowers, borders, symbols, lettering, foliage and stars, all with a fantastical twist.

Fantasy art is both an ancient and a vast subject area, spanning countries and cultures across the globe. Because of this, design sources and styles are incredibly varied. Artists have created beautiful designs, whether depicted in decorative, realistic or stylised forms, and they are all the more stunning considering that they are figments of their creator's mind. Fantasy designs appear not only in art, but also in architecture, literature, textiles and ceramics, and are as popular as ever due to a recent profusion of films and books on the theme. Inspired by this rich source of material, this book offers patterns, motifs, borders and ideas for your own work. You do not need to be particularly artistic to use the designs. Just photocopy or trace the illustrations and transfer them on to your project pieces. You will soon discover the joy of making something beautiful for yourself or your friends and family.

To inspire you, the first section of the book offers an assortment of craft project ideas designed by Judy Balchin, including a glass-painted mermaid, a paper-mâché star box, and a dragon plaque made using polymer clay. Images have been chosen from the design section of the book to illustrate how the motifs can be used to decorate different surfaces. Here you will find glass painting, metal embossing, parchment craft, and polymer clay work. Full instructions are not given for these items. However, if you feel tempted to create them or are inspired to learn one of the crafts shown in these pages, we offer a full range of technique books, with easy to follow step-by-step instructions, on our website: www.searchpress.com. As your confidence and skills grow, you will discover how enjoyable it is to develop the designs in your own way. Have fun.

The Search Press Team

Opposite
For details of the three projects, turn to page 7 for the Party Mask, page 8 for the Goblin Treasure Chest and page 12 for the Spooky Spell Book Box.

Mermaid

Design, see page 81

A swirling picture frame is the perfect border for this glass-painted mermaid. Once the frame is dismantled, the design is outlined on the glass with black outliner. Vitrail glass paints are used to fill in the sections, as the paint flows easily on to the surface, creating a wonderful water effect. Clear glass paint is used to lighten the colours and to create shading on the wave sections. To add some sparkle, a sheet of glitter paper is placed under the glass before the frame is re-assembled.

Party Mask

Design, see page 26

This ready-made mask is first cut to the shape of the pattern. It is then painted with a dilute PVA glue solution and, while the glue is still wet, layered with paper tissues. As the tissue dries, it creates a wonderful textured surface. The mask is then painted with acrylic paints before being rubbed over with gold wax to highlight the texture. A few punched card stars add a final flourish to this stylish party mask.

Goblin Treasure Chest

Design, see page 23

This humble paper-mâché box is transformed into a mysterious Goblin Treasure Chest with just a few paints, some outliner paste and metallic wax. The raised detailing is achieving by applying outliner paste, in swirling, freehand patterns, on to the chest. Gems are pushed into the outliner paste while it is still wet. When dry, the whole chest is then painted with metallic acrylic paint, before the cut-out photocopied images are glued into place. Finally, a little gold wax rubbed over the box highlights the detailing.

Right: Top view of the box.

Mini Mask Plaques

Design, see page 21

These fun mini masks are created from polymer clay. The pattern is photocopied, cut out and laid on top of a sheet of rolled out clay. The clay is then cut out with a scalpel and the features are built up to create a three-dimensional look. After baking in the oven, the plaques are painted with brightly coloured acrylic paint.

Silhouette Halloween Cat Card

Design, page 24

Creating a silhouette is easy and can produce stunning results. The central cat design is transferred on to black paper. Using a scalpel, the cat's body is cut out first , followed by the inner features and detailing. A vibrant coloured card backing, a border of star-studded paper plus a few gold star decorations creates a dramatic effect for your Halloween celebrations.

Opposite

Beaded Phoenix Book Cover

Design, see page 96

This phoenix design is perfect as a centrepiece for this fantasy book cover. The design is transferred on to the cover and outlined with gold outliner paste. When dry, it is painted with acrylic paints. Gold wax is rubbed over the design before the central panel is decorated with small beads.

Below:
This book box has a secret opening – the perfect hiding place for your most precious possessions.

Spooky Spell Book Box

Design, page 17

Have fun creating your very own spell book box using this spooky design. This paper-mâché box is moulded to look like a book…just right for hiding your treasures! The pattern is photocopied and the edges are torn before it is soaked in tea to give it an aged appearance. It is then glued to the front of the box which has been painted cream. Coloured pencils are used to add a little colour before the edges of the book are rubbed with gold wax and decorated with lettered tape.

Dragon Plaque

Design, page 84

This dramatic dragon plaque is created from polymer clay. The design is first outlined on to card. When dry it is pressed on to a sheet of rolled out polymer clay to create an indented design in the clay. A hanging hole is cut at the top of the plaque. The clay is then baked and painted with acrylic paints before being rubbed over with metallic wax. Simply thread some ribbon or leather cord through the hole to hang your plaque.

Opposite

Sophisticated Star Box

Design, see page 86

A plain paper-mâché star-shaped box is the starting point for this sophisticated container. Torn pieces of silver tissue paper are glued over the surface to give it texture. It is then rubbed over with aquamarine metallic wax. The stars and circles are punched from silver card and glued to the box to create a swirling cascade.

Toadstool Bottle

Design, see page 52

Add a fun design to a plain glass bottle with some outliner paste, glitter and glass paints. Carbon paper is used to transfer the design on to the bottle. It is then outlined with black outliner paste. The area beneath the toadstools and the toadstool spots are painted with clear glass paint and sprinkled with glitter. When dry, the excess glitter is removed before the toadstools are painted with coloured glass paints.

Metal Embossed Bird Card

Design, see page 32

Gold metal foil is used to create this sumptuous card. The design is first photocopied to the required size and taped to the back of the foil. It is then traced over with an embossing tool and cut out. The embossed panel is finally glued to the centre of a gold base card which is layered with green papers and decorated with sequin stars.

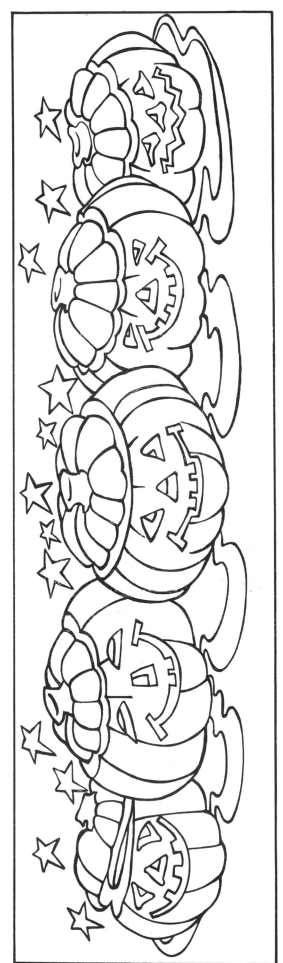

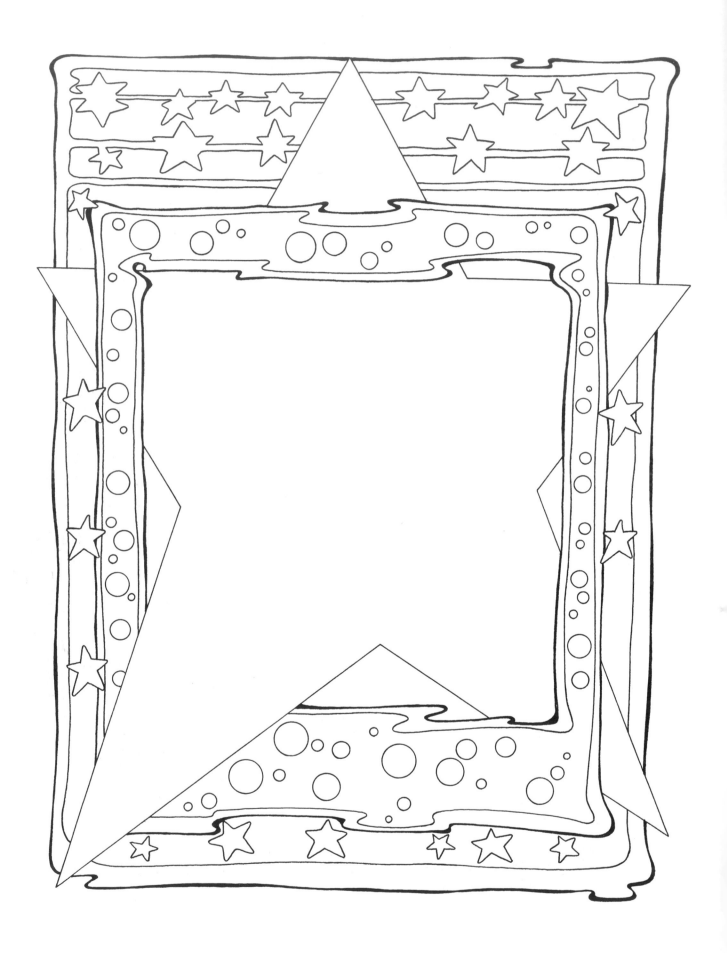

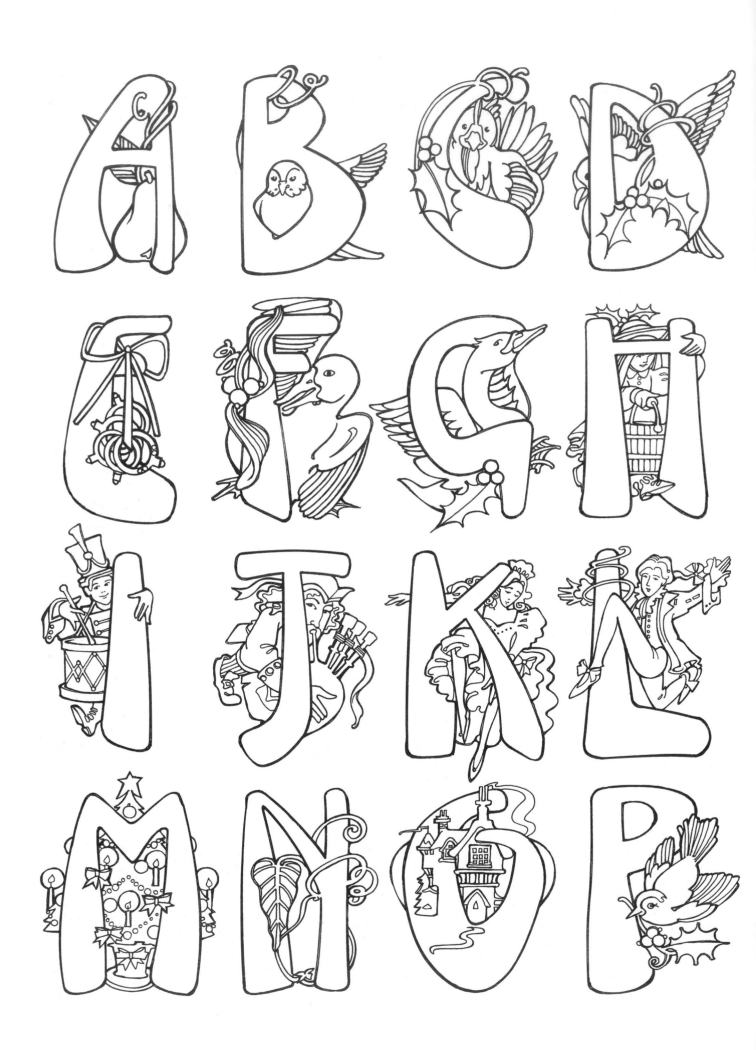

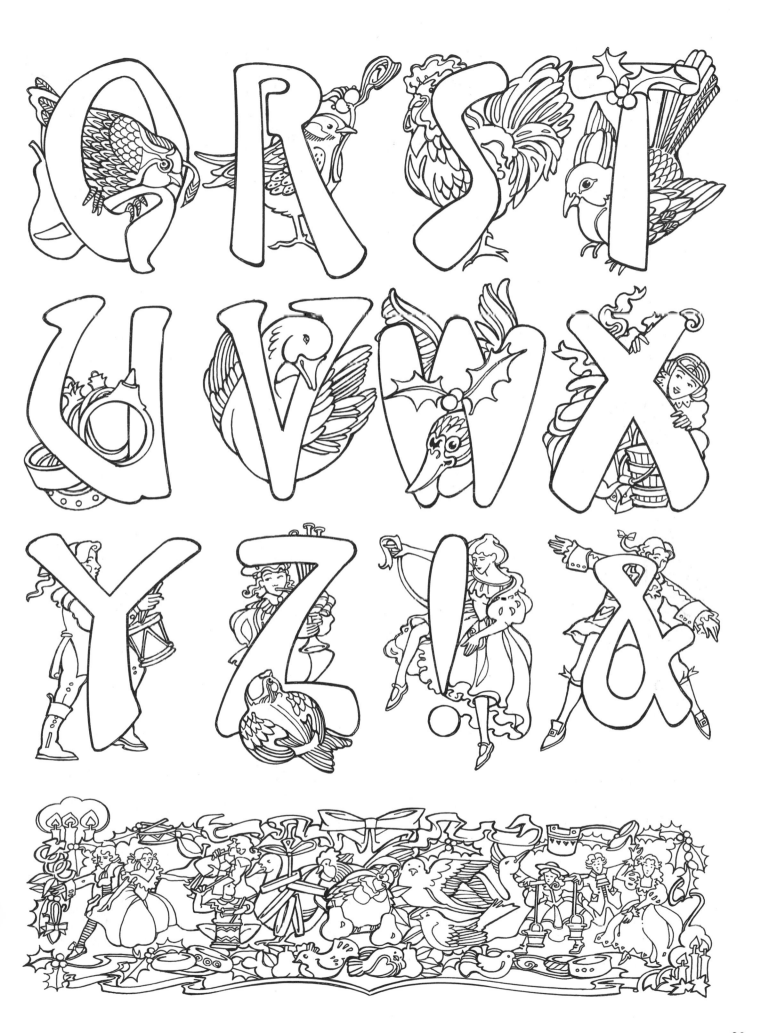

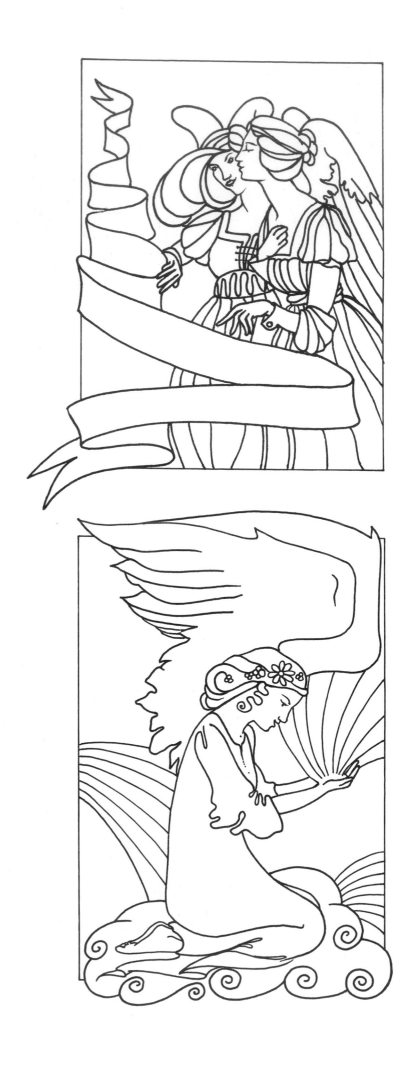

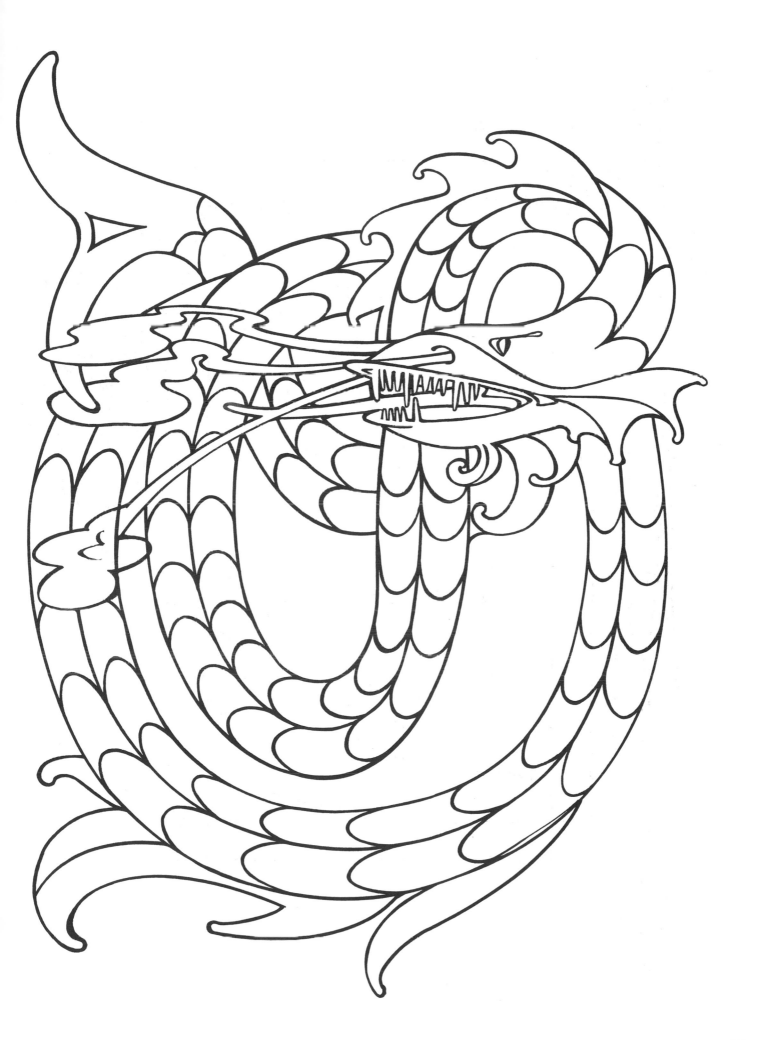